Puddle Jumpers
Fun Weather Projects for Kids

Jennifer Storey Gillis

Illustrations by Patti Delmonte

A Storey Publishing Book
Storey Communications, Inc.

*The mission of Storey Communications is to serve our customers
by publishing practical information that encourages personal independence
in harmony with the environment.*

Edited by Pamela Lappies and Anna Kirwan
Cover design by Susan Bernier
Cover and interior drawings by Patti Delmonte
Text design by Wanda Harper Joyce and Susan Bernier
Text production by Susan Bernier

Printed in Canada by Interglobe, inc.
10 9 8 7 6 5 4 3 2 1

**Other books in this series by Jennifer Storey Gillis and
illustrated by Patti Delmonte**

*In a Pumpkin Shell
An Apple a Day!
Hearts and Crafts
Green Beans & Tambourines
Tooth Truth*

Library of Congress Cataloging-in-Publication Data

Gillis, Jennifer Storey, 1967–
    Puddle jumpers : fun weather projects for kids / Jennifer Storey
Gillis; drawings by Patti Delmonte
        p.   cm.
    "Storey Publishing Book."
    Summary: Presents experiments, activities, and surprising facts
related to weather.
    ISBN 0-88266-938-9 (pb : alk. paper)
    1. Weather — Study and teaching — Activity programs —
Juvenile literature. 2. Meteorology — Study and teaching —
Activity programs — Juvenile literature. 3. Science projects —
Juvenile literature. [1. Weather — Experiments. 2. Experiments.
3. Science projects.] I. Delmonte, Patti, ill.   II. Title.
QC981.5.G55   1996
551.5'078 — dc20   96-18320
                                                              CIP
                                                              AC

Table of Contents

Turn the page for more fun!

Are You a Puddle Jumper?

Do you love looking out the window to see what kind of day it is? Do you smile on a sunny day, and eagerly pull on your favorite boots at the first sign of rain? Can you hardly wait to get out the door — no matter what the weather? If you answered Yes! to these questions, you are a Puddle Jumper!

Puddle Jumpers like all kinds of weather. They use all their senses to notice, explore, and enjoy the day around them — no matter what the weather is. So grab your raincoat, mittens, and sunglasses — you never know what the day has in store!

What Is Weather?

Weather is the snow that falls, the rain that makes puddles, and the wind that flies a kite. In this book we will explore the kinds of weather below — and more!

Sunshine — The sun is a star that gives us energy and light, warms the soil and sea, and helps plants grow.

Clouds — You see them in most kinds of weather: puffy mountains and feathery wisps that float in the sky. They are made of warm air and tiny water droplets.

Rain — Water in the clouds turns into heavy droplets, and rain falls. It can cause rainbows.

Snow — These soft white ice crystals that fall from cold air often pile up deep.

Wind — Moving air that can blow in any direction, wind is sometimes gentle, often rough, and it plays a part in every weather forecast.

What Good Is Weather?

Nature uses seasons to time changes in all growing things — plants, animals, and people. Our bodies and even our moods react to sunshine and to cold. We couldn't grow crops for food or wood for building without the changing weather.

Animals use weather to give their bodies signals. When the weather turns cold, bears take nice, long snoozes. Birds fly to where the weather is good for their young. Wild animals rely on the right weather conditions for finding fresh drinking water and food.

Weather Words

Lots of weather vocabulary is used in the news, and Puddle Jumpers need to know these terms. Read on, and you will be prepared for any kind of weather!

Meteorologist — a scientist who studies the weather and makes forecasts.

Forecast — a description of what the weather will be.

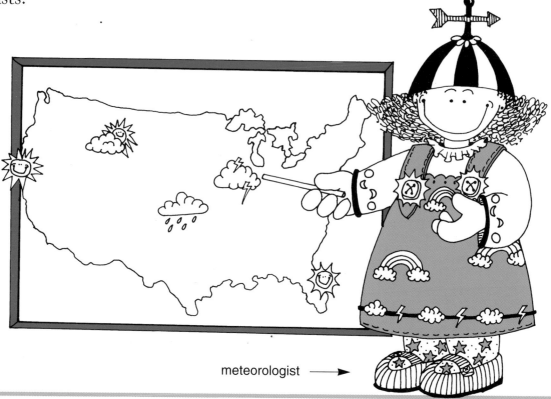

meteorologist ──▶

Precipitation — rain, snow, mist, hail, or any other kind of water coming from the sky.

Evaporation — water changes into tiny particles and disappears into the air.

Thermometer — an instrument that measures the air's temperature.

Cold front — the edge of the cold air that is moving into warmer air; sometimes causes precipitation.

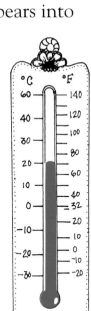

thermometer

Warm front — the edge of the warm air that is moving into cold air; sometimes brings fair weather.

Drought — a long time with little or no rain.

Barometer — an instrument used to predict the weather. When the barometer shows changes in the air, we know the weather will change soon, too.

barometer

5

Gloves or Galoshes?
Lore for Predicting the Weather

What would you do if there were no weather reports on the TV or radio? Before there were meteorologists, how did people know what kind of weather to expect?

To learn about the changing weather, people have always watched animals, clouds, the moon — everything in nature. You have probably heard some of these rhymes and phrases.

The next time you see the weather changing, use your powers of observation to see if this natural "lore" works.

◆ Spiders stop spinning their webs when rain is coming.

Home Sweet Home

Bee it ever so Hum-m-m-ble!

- Bees tend to stay inside their hives just before it rains.

- *Swallows fly high: clear blue sky; Swallows fly low: rain we shall know.*

- Toadstools (mushrooms) often appear before it rains.

- A ring around the moon means a storm is coming.

- If corn husks are thicker than usual, that means a tough winter is ahead.

- *Red sky at night, sailors delight. Red sky at morning, sailors take warning.* (This means, if the sunset is reddish, the weather will be good the next day. If the sky's red in the morning, though — watch out!)

- When cows lie down during light rain, it will clear soon.

- March comes in like a lion and goes out like a lamb.

7

A Weather Calendar

Puddle Jumpers don't just watch the weather. They keep track of it!
Here is a way to record what you find outside every day.

WHAT YOU WILL NEED

▶ Ruler
▶ Crayons or markers
▶ Poster board

Sun	Mon	Tue	Wed	Thur	Fri	Sat
1	2	3	4	5	6	7
8	9	10	11	12	13	14

1. Use the ruler and a marker or a crayon to draw the boxes for the days of the month on the poster board. Put the days across the top. Write the date in small numbers in the corner of each box.

2. Hang the calendar next to a window.

3. Each day look out the window and observe the weather. In the box for that day, draw the proper picture.

4. Add other information, too, such as temperature outside or the amount of snow that fell on the ground.

Reliable Rain Gauge

1. Ask your grown-up helper to cut off the top part of the soda bottle. Turn it upside down and place it back inside the bottle. Tape it in place. (Be sure to throw away the screw top — you don't need it for this project.)

2. Take your rain gauge outside, away from the house or garage, to an open spot in your yard. Place the rocks or bricks around it so it won't fall over in the wind and rain.

3. When rain or snow falls, it will be caught in the bottle. Measure it with a ruler at the end of every day. Keep track of your results and compare rainfall on different days.

- ◆ Remember — a day is 24 hours, so try to measure the rainfall at the same time every day.
- ◆ After you measure and record the rainfall, dump out the collected water and start again.

Sunny Day Stroll

On the next beautiful, sunny day, put down your basketball and hold off on your jump rope. Puddle Jumpers use their senses to observe the weather. What would you see, hear, smell, taste, and feel if you were in this picture?

Now use your senses on your own Sunny Day Stroll!

Look around you. What are different animals and plants doing? Do people look hot? Is the sunshine glistening on the snow? Do you see shadows?

Listen for sounds around you. Do you hear lawn mowers or rakes swishing up leaves? Can you hear wind? Are there birds singing?

Smell the air on a sunny day. Flowers and leaves are most fragrant when they're warm. If it's a cold, winter day, how does the air make your nose feel? Sniff away!

Taste the flavors of a sunny day. Are there foods you get to eat only when the sun is shining? Try strawberries or sugar peas straight from the garden.

Touch things the sun has been shining on. Does your dog's coat feel different? How about the stone wall behind the house, or the top layer of sand at the beach? Compare the water in a puddle with water from the hose. Which is warmer?

Sun Safety

Sun safety habits are important even when there are clouds and shadows. Some of the sun's rays can sneak through and burn your skin. Put on sunscreen when you'll be outside, and wear a hat to keep sunlight off your face.

11

Flowerpot Sundials

Use shadow and sun to tell the time.

WHAT YOU WILL NEED

▶ Flowerpot
▶ Black marker
▶ Stick or pencil that is twice the height of the pot and fits through the bottom hole
▶ Small piece of clay

1 Take your materials outside to a sunny spot that won't be bothered by dogs, cats, or baby sisters! You can put your sundial on pavement or right on the grass.

2 Turn the pot over and stick the pencil through the hole. If it is on the lawn, push it right into the dirt, and if it is on another type of surface, use the clay to stick it to the ground. (This is so the pencil won't lean and make your clock tell the wrong time.)

3 Check your clock every hour. Make a small mark on the pot where the pencil's shadow falls. Write the time under the first mark. By the end of the afternoon you will have an easy way to tell the time every sunny day! Leave your sundial in the same place for it to tell the right time day after day.

Sundials of the Past

◆ Sundials were used by the ancient peoples over 4,000 years ago. For example, Egyptian builders planned temples so shadows could be used as clocks and calendars.

◆ In England in the 1600s a sundial was made that not only told the time but also shot off a cannon at noon on every sunny day!

13

Sunny and Shady Seeds

We like sunny days because we can go outside and play. Sun is even more important to plants, which need sunlight in order to make their food. Try this gardening experiment and see how hard it is for a plant to grow in the dark.

WHAT YOU WILL NEED

- Two plastic cups
- Bean seeds
- Enough soil to fill both cups
- Water

1 Pour some water into one cup. Add all the seeds and let them soak overnight. This will help the seeds to open more easily and sprout into plants more quickly.

2 Empty the water and remove the seeds. Put the soil into both cups. Place a bean seed in each. Push it down about 1½ inches and cover it with dirt. Water it carefully — not too much, or the seed will drown before it starts to grow.

3 Put one cup in a sunny window and the other in a dark closet. Check their progress every day. If you water them the same amount, the biggest difference will be that one gets sunlight and the other doesn't. What effect does the sunlight have? How is the plant in the closet different?

More Things to Try

◆ You can try another experiment with plants. Put one in the sun every day and the other in the sun only every other day. What happens? Do they both grow? Are they the same height? Which one is stronger?

◆ Make a chart to keep track of how your plants grow. After your seeds come up, measure the plants daily. Cut string to be the same height as each plant. Tape the string for each plant to a separate piece of paper. Write the date underneath each string.

Sun-Dried Apples

The sun can dry your hair, your clothes on the line, and your wet dog.
Did you know that it can dry your food as well?

· · · · ▸ WHAT YOU WILL NEED ◂ · · · ·

- ▸ 5 sweet-tart apples (such as Empire or Granny Smith)
- ▸ Paring knife for your grown-up helper
- ▸ Pineapple juice
- ▸ Bowl
- ▸ Cookie sheets
- ▸ Cheesecloth

1 Wash your apples well and dry them for your grown-up helper. Ask him to core the apple — to take out the middle. You should be able to see right through the apples when they are done.

2 Have your grown-up helper slice the apple into rings or into ¼-inch-thick wedges. Pour the pineapple juice into the bowl, and soak the apple slices in it for about an hour. This will keep the apples from turning too brown as they dry.

3 Put the apple slices on the cookie sheet and cover them with cheesecloth. Take them out into full sunlight, and stir them every few hours so that all the sides get dried. (Remember to bring the trays inside at night so animals don't get to taste your treats before you do!)

 4 In 2 or 3 days the apples should be dry all the way through. They will be leathery and chewy when they're done, and not crispy at all. Store them in an airtight container, and snack on them as much as you want.

Other Foods the Sun Can Dry

◆ Tomatoes are dried by the sun and used on pizza and with pasta.
◆ Raisins are really dried grapes.
◆ Prunes, apricots, peaches, and other fruit can also be dried.

Sunshine Drippers

On some hot, sunny days you feel as if you are melting. Did you know that ice cubes really do melt away in the sun's heat?

Dripper #1 Put an ice cube on the sidewalk or driveway in the sunlight. Start your stopwatch. How long does it take the cube to melt?

Dripper #2 Put one ice cube in the sun and one in the shade. Start your watch. How much longer does it take the shaded ice cube to melt?

Dripper #3 Put one ice cube in the sun and one in a glass of cold water in the sun. Which will melt faster? Why?

Dripper #4 Guess what will happen if you put one ice cube in the sun and one in a glass of hot water in the sun. Now try it out!

Dripper #5 Put one ice cube outside in the sun, and one inside in a very sunny window. Does one melt faster?

WHAT YOU WILL NEED

- Ice cubes
- Sunny day
- Stopwatch

Radiant Rainbows

Usually we see only the white light of the sun, but when the white light shines through raindrops, it bends and splits up into different wavelengths — the colors we see as the rainbow. Some people remember the rainbow colors and the order they appear in by memorizing this name — **Roy G. Biv**. Those letters stand for Red, Orange, Yellow, Green, Blue, Indigo (dark blue), and Violet.

Rainbow Fun

 Have someone hold a garden hose up high and let the water spray down. With your back toward the sun, look right at the spray. Can you see a little rainbow inside it?

 Look carefully when you blow bubbles — you just might see a rainbow float by!

A Cloudy Day Adventure

Sometimes the weather news says, "Partly cloudy," "Patchy Fog," or maybe even, "Clouds appearing in the afternoon." Does a cloudy day mean indoor play? Not for a Puddle Jumper! What would you see, hear, smell, taste, and feel if you were in this picture?

Now use your senses on your own Cloudy Day Adventure!

Do you find yourself squinting today, or can you easily look up at the sky? Are there shadows on the ground? What are people wearing? Is anyone carrying an umbrella?

What do you hear? Do the birds sing as cheerfully when the sun isn't out? Are the bugs buzzing? If the clouds get thick and dark and you think it might rain, do the noises change at all? Do cars and trains sound louder than on a sunny day?

Can you smell rain coming? Or are the smells still hot and sunshiny, as if the clouds might be covering the sun for only a moment? When you breathe in, do you feel cool air or warm air in your nose?

What do you taste today? It might depend on the temperature as well as the cloud cover. Does lemonade sound as good on a cloudy day as it does on a bright sunny one? How about chicken noodle soup? You may be surprised!

Things outside may be cool to the touch today, since the clouds block the sun from them. If it is very foggy, you can actually reach out and touch those ground clouds! Sometimes fog is so thick it seems as if you could scoop it up into your arms! Can you see your hand at arm's length? Does the fog make the grass or the windows wet? If you're in the fog for a while, it might even make your hair feel wet.

21

All Kinds of Clouds

Some parts of the country get more clouds than others, but clouds are found in weather patterns everywhere. There are names for different kinds of clouds.

Stratus are low, gray, "rainy day" clouds.

Cumulus are the white, fluffy, "cotton ball" clouds.

Cirrus are high, wispy clouds. (The name is Latin for "curl of hair.")

Cloud Lore

A cloud may provide rain, or shade, or a changing shape to look at. If the temperature is cold enough, it may even bring snow. People have always watched and wondered about clouds. Here is some weather wisdom they have gathered.

◆ When clouds look like rocks
    and towers,
the earth will have many showers.

◆ When woolly clouds (cumulus)
    come this way,
not rain or snow will spoil the day.

◆ Shiny (sunny) morning, cloudy day;
cloudy morning, shiny day.

◆ Woolly sheep in the sky (cumulus)
bunched together like sheep will
bring rain by and by.

Even Mother Goose had something to say about a cloudy morning!

One misty moisty morning
When cloudy was the weather,
I met with an old man
Clothed all in leather;
From his foot unto his chin,
Saying: "How-de-do and how-de-do,
And how-de-do again."

Creative Clouds

Use your imagination and step into a cloudy day. Is that an elephant in the sky?

WHAT YOU WILL NEED

- ▶ Writing paper and a pencil
- ▶ Construction paper
- ▶ Glue
- ▶ Scissors
- ▶ Cotton balls

 1 Watch the clouds as they drift by outside your window. What do they look like? You might be surprised at the familiar shapes you see. You might see a pirate ship, a train, or maybe even an ice cream cone!

 **2** With paper, pencil, and plenty of imagination, write a story about your shapes. It might be fun to have your friends look at the same clouds and write their own stories, and then share them when you are done. Were you looking at the same clouds?

 Once you finish your story, make a collage to illustrate it. Use a piece of construction paper as the background, and draw a scene from your story with your crayons. Or you can cut shapes from paper and glue them on. Save the cotton for your special cloud shape. You can pull it and bunch it any way you want before gluing it to the paper.

 Share your story and picture with your parents and friends. You can even collect your cloud stories and make them into a cloud book!

Kitchen Clouds

Watch your grown-up helper make clouds for you right in the kitchen.
Never *do it by yourself!*

• • WHAT YOU WILL NEED • •

- Grown-up helper
- Stove
- Pot with lid
- Water

1 Have your grown-up helper put water in the pot and set it on a burner with the lid on. Turn on the stove. When the water comes to a rolling boil, you are ready to make clouds.

2 Carefully stand back as your grown-up helper slowly lifts the lid straight up. What do you see? A cloud forms under the lid and then disappears. Put the top on and lift it again; another cloud should appear.

Fascinating Fog

Fog is really stratus clouds floating close to the ground. Walking through fog is like walking through a cloud — you can actually feel the droplets of water.

You may have seen a lighthouse at the seashore. It is a tower with a powerful light on top that warns ships and boats that they are close to land and should sail carefully. Light-houses are especially important in foggy weather, when it may be impossible to see the shore. Some also have foghorns that send out a booming noise — if the light doesn't cut through the fog, the foghorn will.

Fog Words

◆ A **fog bank** is a large area of fog, usually seen near the sea. It may be clear all around the fog.
◆ Sailors call a bright spot in the middle of a fog bank a **fogdog**.
◆ A **fogbow** looks like a rainbow but has only yellow, white, and orange colors in it.

Running in the Rain

Rain, Rain, Go Away, Come again some other day! Have you ever heard that little song and said to yourself that you didn't want the rain to go away? You are truly a Puddle Jumper! What would you see, hear, smell, taste, and feel if you were in this picture?

Now use your senses as you go Running in the Rain!

Your eyes may get raindrops in them as you look to the sky today! Are the usual animals around, or do you see different ones today? Has it been raining a long time? How can you tell?

What do you hear? Is the rain soft and steady? Is it hard and fast? What sounds does rain make on different objects — trash cans, the grass, a puddle, the roof?

Does a rainy day smell different? What does the grass smell like? And the dirt? Does the air smell clean?

What does rain taste like? A few drops on your tongue is plenty to recognize it. What do you want to eat on a rainy day — how does grilled cheese and tomato soup sound?

Is it a warm rain or a cold rain? Are things outside slippery? How about the road, the sidewalk, your lawn? Is there mud to stomp in? Are there puddles to jump? How does your dog's fur feel?

Rain Records

How much rain falls in a year where you live? Here are some amazing rainfall records:

◆ On March 15, 1952, on an island in the Indian Ocean, it rained 73½ inches in one day.

◆ In July 1961 it rained 366 inches in Assam, India.

◆ In Atacama, Chile (South America), 400 years passed without rain.

◆ Hawaii averages 460 inches of rain a year.

29

The Water Cycle

Did you know the earth has been using the same water over and over for billions of years?

1. Water in ponds, lakes, and oceans evaporates as the sun warms it, turns into vapor (steam), and rises into the air.

2. The vapor in air is invisible. Warm air can hold lots of water vapor, but as it rises and hits cooler air, it forms droplets that cling together, making clouds. Now we can see the water again.

3. As water droplets cling to each other and to dust particles in the sky, they get heavier and heavier. Soon they cannot stay up anymore and fall to the ground. Rain! It falls to earth to water the forests and crops and to fill ponds, lakes, rivers, and oceans.

Who Needs It?

When your game gets rained out or the class picnic is cancelled, you may wonder, who needs this? But before you wish for no rain, remember:

◆ Rain keeps plants and animals alive. No rain would mean no fresh drinking water — and no food crops could grow, either.

◆ Rain cools things off. Have you ever been so hot you were dreaming of rain?

◆ Rain is part of the wonderful water cycle. No rain would mean no ponds to fish in, no lakes to swim in, and no oceans to sail.

Who Needs Water?

Lightning and Thunder

Most rain falls softly, but not a rainstorm accompanied by lightning and thunder! You will see flashes and hear booms. What are lightning and thunder?

Lightning

Lightning is the release of electricity that builds up in a cloud. Most of the time, lightning stays inside a cloud and never even reaches the earth. When it does leave a cloud, it travels through the air until it contacts something tall — then it "strikes." Flagpoles, tall buildings, and trees are often hit by lightning.

Thunder

Lightning heats the air, making it expand very quickly. The expanding air makes a shock wave travel through the air, and the shock wave is thunder. Light travels faster than sound, so a flash of lightning reaches us before the sound of thunder.

Did you know?

There are six kinds of lightning: forked, beaded, ball, heat, sheet, and ribbon lightning all strike around us.

Benjamin Franklin's experiments with a kite and a key proved that lightning is electricity.

Every square mile of southern Florida gets struck by lightning about 40 times a year.

When you see a lightning flash, start counting. Every 5 seconds you count before you hear thunder means the lightning is 1 mile away. So if it takes 10 seconds for the thunder to boom, the lightning is 2 miles away.

Thunderstorm Safety

◆ Stay inside if you can, and watch safely from a dry spot. If you get caught out in the open, crouch down on the ground and stay away from metal and tall objects — like trees or flagpoles.

◆ Avoid talking on the telephone. Call back later.

◆ Don't take a bath or shower until the storm is over.

33

Picking Up Puddles

Have you ever wondered where puddles go after the rain stops and the sun comes out? **Evaporation** is the weather word that explains it. Puddles are dried up by the sun and change from a liquid (water) to a vapor (steam). We can't see, touch, or taste it, but it's in the air all around us.

 How would you measure a puddle? Think up as many ideas as you can for different ways to measure the one you just splashed in. Ask others to think, too — you'll get some great answers.

How long does it take for a puddle to disappear? Find a puddle and trace around it with chalk. Next, write down what time it is. Check your puddle every hour (or every day, in some cases) and see how it's doing. Every time it shrinks a bit, trace its new shape with the chalk. Be sure you really keep your eye on it as it gets close to evaporating completely. You want to note the time again, and then figure out how long it took. Do big puddles take longer to evaporate than little puddles? Do puddles take longer to disappear in certain kinds of weather?

Float some leaves or a rubber ducky in a puddle. How shallow a puddle can you use? What kinds of things float? Does a penny, a feather, or a Ping-Pong ball float? Make a list; predict what you think will float, then check your predictions.

Rain Painting

Start this rainy day art project indoors but finish it off in the rain. Then use this picture to make a card for a friend who's feeling "under the weather."

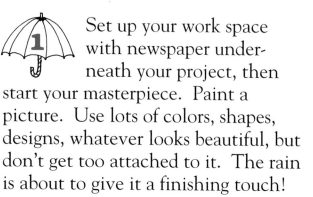

••• **WHAT YOU WILL NEED** •••

- ▶ Old newspaper
- ▶ Piece of white construction paper
- ▶ Watercolors or washable markers
- ▶ Water
- ▶ Brush
- ▶ A rainy day

1 Set up your work space with newspaper underneath your project, then start your masterpiece. Paint a picture. Use lots of colors, shapes, designs, whatever looks beautiful, but don't get too attached to it. The rain is about to give it a finishing touch!

2 Put on your raincoat and take your picture outside. Hold it in the rain for just a few seconds. The raindrops will splash the color and add their own creative touch. Your picture will dry with the rain's fingerprints all over it!

Baked Raindrops

*These baked goodies aren't for eating, but you can see the size
and shape of raindrops this way.*

1 Sprinkle flour onto the cookie sheet so that it is about ½ inch deep.

2 Take the tray out into the rain for a few seconds, and then bring it back inside for baking.

3 Have your grown-up helper put the tray in the oven and bake the raindrops for 30 minutes. Let them cool for at least 15 minutes.

4 Sift the flour through a colander or sieve. What you should have left in the bottom are baked raindrops! Are they all the same size?

- Flour
- Cookie sheet
- A rainy day
- Grown-up helper
- Oven preheated to 350°F
- Sieve or colander

37

Snowy Day Stomp

Taking a walk (or a stomp!) on a sunny, snowy day is the perfect way to enjoy winter weather. What would you see, hear, smell, taste, and feel if you were in this picture?

Now use your senses on your own Snowy Day Stomp!

If it is a sunny, snowy day, you might need to squint. The sun reflecting off the snow is very bright! Can you see individual snowflakes? Animal footprints? Who do you see? What expressions are on their faces? (They might be different, depending on whose face you look at — the man shoveling, or the kids sledding, for instance!)

Sometimes things sound clearer in cold, snowy air. Can you hear things that are far away? Are snowblowers whirring, shovels scraping, chains on tires clinking?

How does your nose feel, inside and out? If it is very cold, you might need a scarf or ski mask to keep it covered. Is there anything in nature to smell at this time of year, or is everything covered up? Do you smell woodburning stoves? Evergreen trees?

Watch your breath on a snowy day — you will be able to make your own clouds! Be careful what you taste on a freezing cold day, though — sticking out your tongue can turn it frosty. Don't touch your tongue or any part of your mouth to any sort of metal (a skate blade, a saucer, or a sled for example). It will hurt and could cause injury. Save your taste buds for hot chocolate and cookies when you come inside!

You may have a different sense of touch with your mittens on! Feel snow with your bare hands, too: is it crunchy, smooth, great for snowballs? How long does it take for your hand to melt the snow? Do your hands stay warmer in mittens or gloves?

A Snowflake Grows

When water vapor in a cloud hits freezing air, it forms ice crystals that fall to the ground. Now you have snow! Every snowflake has basically six sides, yet each one is unique. Once a water drop in a cloud freezes, other drops cling to it, and that is what makes the ice crystal a star-shaped flake. The more water vapor a cloud has in it, the bigger each snowflake will be. If a cloud has very little water vapor in it, the snowflakes will be smaller.

Did you know?

How much does it usually snow each year where you live? Here are some amazing snowfall records:

* Silver Lake, Colorado, had 75 inches of snow in a single day! And it was in April!

* A 6-day snow storm in California produced 189 inches of snow.

* Valdez, Alaska, gets 50 to 60 feet of snow each winter.

Snow Painting

*You can go outside and create a masterpiece even when the weather is cold!
Ask your grown-up helper before you do this painting — it will
definitely change the face of the beautiful white snow.*

1. Fill each spray bottle with water and a few drops of food coloring. If you only have one bottle, use one color at a time, rinse the sprayer, and fill it again.

2. Find a good spot to paint. Then, just spray your colors onto the snow. Your design will disappear as soon as it snows again, and you will have a new canvas to decorate.

◆ Write a message for your parents or friends. Be certain to do it in a place they'll be sure to pass by.

◆ If you want to erase part of your picture before it snows again, just shovel some snow on top.

◆ Write your name in the snow — use a different color for every letter!

41

Snow Sculpting

If you have good snow for packing, the weather is right for snow sculpting! There are plenty of things to make. Just use your imagination and jump right in.

Some ideas to get you started:

Snowhorse — Make two large snowballs and put them next to each other. Put a smaller snowball on one end of one of the big ones. Scoop a saddle from the top of the other one. Add a branch or a whisk broom for a tail and ride 'em cowboy!

Snow family — Make a big snowball for the bottom, a medium-sized ball for the body, and a smaller one for the head. Add a face, and name your new friend. Make a snow-spouse and some kids.

Snow angel — Lie down in the snow and sweep your arms and legs across the snow as far as they will go. Do this 3 or 4 times. Then carefully stand up and see what you've created!

Snow furniture — Make a huge chair to sit in, or a giant snow bed. Pile up the snow and then shape it. You could make an entire living room — how about a lamp on a table?

43

Build a Snow Fort

There's nothing more fun than creating a hideout in the snow —
as long as you make the sky your ceiling!

• • • WHAT YOU WILL NEED • • •

- ▶ Sturdy scissors
- ▶ One-gallon milk jug
- ▶ Snow
- ▶ Mittened hands
- ▶ Shovels

 1 Ask a grown-up to cut away the top part of an empty milk jug to make a snow scoop. Be sure not to cut off the handle.

 2 Find a large pile of snow. Check the edges of your driveway after the snow plow has been there for already piled snow.

 3 Use your snow scoop, shovel, and hands to dig away the snow. Make an area big enough to sit and play in. Build the walls high by using your scoop and packing the snow into place on top of the walls. Get as many friends to help as you can. Many hands make light work!

4 It is very important for you to leave the ceiling open. You must be able to see the sky when you're inside your fort. Snow is very heavy and could hurt you if it fell on your head. Make your fort more of a maze. You can hide behind the walls and pretend it is a mighty fortress!

5 Remember, every fort will be different. There are no rules when it comes to building in the snow except for leaving the top open. Make several rooms, flatten the floors, make windows, or make a snow throne. Whatever you do will look terrific and be fun!

Experimenting with Snow

Try some of these ideas on your winter vacation or on your next snow day!

 Take a magnifying glass and a piece of black paper or cloth outside when snow is falling. After the paper or cloth gets cold, catch snowflakes on it and examine their shapes and sizes. Are they all really different?

 How long does it take a 1-cup scoop of snow to melt after you take it inside? Does it take exactly twice as long for a 2-cup scoop?

 What happens when you pour hot water on snow? What happens when you pour cold water on it? Are you surprised by the results?

Did you know?

◆ In Native American lore, the full moon in February is called the "Snow Moon" because blizzards often strike then.

◆ "Blackberry Winter" is the cold spell that comes in May after there has already been a little warm weather.

◆ The Eskimos, or Inuits, have 12 different names for snow.

Paper Flakes

Even if you don't have a snowy day outside, you can make these paper snowflakes.

··· WHAT YOU WILL NEED ···

▸ Thin, white paper
▸ Scissors

1 Start with a square of paper and fold it diagonally so that it looks like a fancy napkin.

2 Hold it with the long side of the triangle at the bottom. Fold the bottom corners up across each other so that their points stick out almost as high as the top point.

3 Trim the top edges of your paper so that it is shaped like a diamond. Make sure that you cut through every layer of the paper.

4 You're ready to begin! Make little cuts and snips along the sides and corners of the diamond, being careful not to cut all the way across. Carefully unfold it and your snowflake will appear! Tape these beautiful flakes to the window or string them together as a wintery garland to decorate a room.

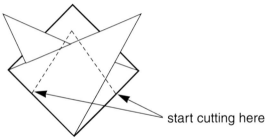

start cutting here

Snow Sleuth — Tracking Animals in the Snow

The next time it snows, look for animal tracks. You may be surprised at what you find! Here's your first mystery to solve: How did the squirrel in this picture get into the tree without leaving tracks all the way to the tree trunk?

Dogs' pawprints can be anywhere from 1 inch to 4 inches across. They have 4 "toes" and a heel pad and tiny claw marks.

Cats leave prints that are a little more than 1 inch across. They look like a dog's paws except they are smaller and do not leave claw marks. Cats walk with their claws inside their paws!

A fox's pawprint looks like that of a dog, except that the toes are farther apart. Also, foxes walk in a straighter line than dogs do.

Deer make heart-shaped footprints. The point of the heart shows the direction the deer is moving in. Since deer are heavier than smaller animals, their prints will be deeper.

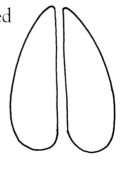

Rabbits have big hind feet that are about 3 inches long and smaller front feet about 1 inch long. Their tracks are funny because the front prints are found behind the back pawprints because of the way they hop. They land with their front feet and swing their back feet ahead of the front feet before pushing off again.

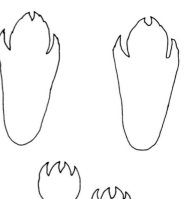

49

Frost

Have you ever gotten up in the morning and looked out your window to see a thin coat of white on the grass? It's not snow or frozen rain. It's frost. Frost happens when the temperature of the ground is below 32°F and water or dew on the grass freezes. When the sun comes out and the ground warms up, the frost disappears.

◆ Frost kills plants by freezing the water inside the leaves. If there is a frost warning for your area, cover your plants with old sheets, bedspreads, or towels to keep them warm. The warmer they are, the harder it is for frost to form.

◆ If you *do* get light frost on your plants, you can carefully spray water on them to melt the frost before it harms the plants.

Have you ever heard of Jack Frost? He is an imaginary character said to visit on chilly mornings to decorate the ground and windows with his feathery white artwork. He's also said to "nip at your nose" when it's cold out!

Ice

Ice forms when water cools to below 32°F. You might see it outdoors on a pond, on a puddle, or even coming from the sky as sleet. It's fun to skate on, but it can be very slippery for walking and driving.

Icicles

Icicles are the beautiful hanging crystals that form where water drips continuously. They come in all different sizes because of how they form. When water drips off a roof or branch and the air is very cold, the drops of water immediately start to freeze. The more water drops that freeze, the longer the icicle becomes.

Never stand under an icicle — it may fall and hurt you!

51

Walking in the Wind

Wind is moving air. As warm air rises into the sky, cooler air rushes over to fill its space. This rush is called the wind. A windy day is a treat for Puddle Jumpers, as long as it isn't too cold or rainy. If you were in this picture with these Puddle Jumpers, what would you see, hear, smell, taste, and feel?

Now use your senses on your own Walk in the Wind!

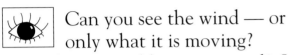 Can you see the wind — or only what it is moving? What do you see blowing around? Is it strong enough to rustle the leaves? Or blow flags out straight? What is the smoke over chimneys doing?

Does the wind howl? Or whistle? What kind of sounds does it make in the trees? Around corners of your house? Is it strong enough to rattle the glass in windows?

Can you smell the wind? Can you smell other things in the wind? If you live near the seashore, can you smell salt water in the air? How about the cow pasture down the road?

You'd better keep your mouth closed as the wind rushes by — you never know what might blow into it! If you do open up for a minute, what does the wind feel like inside? Does it taste like anything?

Can you feel the wind? Is it warm or cold? Fan your hands in front of your face and see if they can make a wind of their own.

Wind Chill

To find the wind chill factor, a meteorologist must know the temperature and how fast the wind is blowing. The faster the wind is blowing, the colder it makes the air feel. So bundle up on cold, windy days.

Weather Vanes

Farmers put weather vanes on top of their barns to learn the direction the wind is blowing from.

- ▶ Drinking straw
- ▶ Little piece of thin cardboard
- ▶ Glue
- ▶ Straight pin
- ▶ Pencil with an eraser
- ▶ Crayon or marker
- ▶ Flower pot
- ▶ Dirt or sand
- ▶ 2 ice-pop sticks cut in half
- ▶ Magnetic compass
- ▶ Grown-up helper

1. Have your grown-up helper cut a little slit at both ends of the straw. Cut the cardboard into a large triangle and a small triangle. Glue the point of the big triangle into the slit at one end of the straw. Glue the bottom side of the small triangle into the slit at the other end.

2. Color the pointer of the straw with your marker. Carefully stick the straight pin through the straw about 2½ inches away from the end, and then into the pencil eraser.

54

3. Fill the flowerpot with sand or dirt. Put the pencil into the sand or dirt. It should stand straight, with the straw end up.

4. Take the pieces of ice-pop stick and write N, E, S, and W on the rounded ends. Looking down at your pot, pretend that it's a clock and stick the N in at 12:00, the E at 3:00, the S at 6:00, and the W at 9:00.

5. Take your compass weather vane outside, away from buildings. Put both on the ground. Turn your compass until the arrow and the N line up. Now turn your weather vane so that the N is in the same direction as the N on your compass. When the wind blows, it will be coming from the direction the arrow is pointing in.

Weather vanes are often made of metal, in the shape of animals. Read this poem about a cow weather vane.

> *A cow with its tail to the west*
> *Makes weather the best,*
> *A cow with its tail to the east*
> *Makes weather the least.*

In other words, winds coming from the west bring good weather, and those coming from the east usually bring storms!

Wind Chimes

Hang these beautiful chimes on your porch or in front of a window.
Every time the weather stirs, you will hear wind music.

• • • • WHAT YOU WILL NEED • • • •

▸ 2 sticks about the same size
▸ String
▸ Tape
▸ Objects to make the chime
(paper cups, shells, buttons)

1. Hold the 2 sticks so they cross in the middle and make an X. Tie them with the string so they don't slide around. This will be the base for your chimes. Now, tie a piece of string about 1 foot long to the X in the sticks. You can use this to hang the wind chimes when you're finished.

2. Hang various lengths of string from the sticks. Make sure that some strings are just about the same length, so that the objects dangling from the ends will bang together when the wind blows.

3. Using your tape, carefully attach "chimes" to the ends of the strings. (If you use paper cups, be sure that the bottoms are facing up: that gives a richer tone.) Use whatever you have available that you think might work. It must be light enough to hang in the air and noisy enough to make a sound. Beach glass or bottle caps will work just fine. Jingle bells will be fantastic!

4. Hang your chimes in the wind and listen. Each kind of object you hang will have a different sound. And just wait until you get a really gusty day!

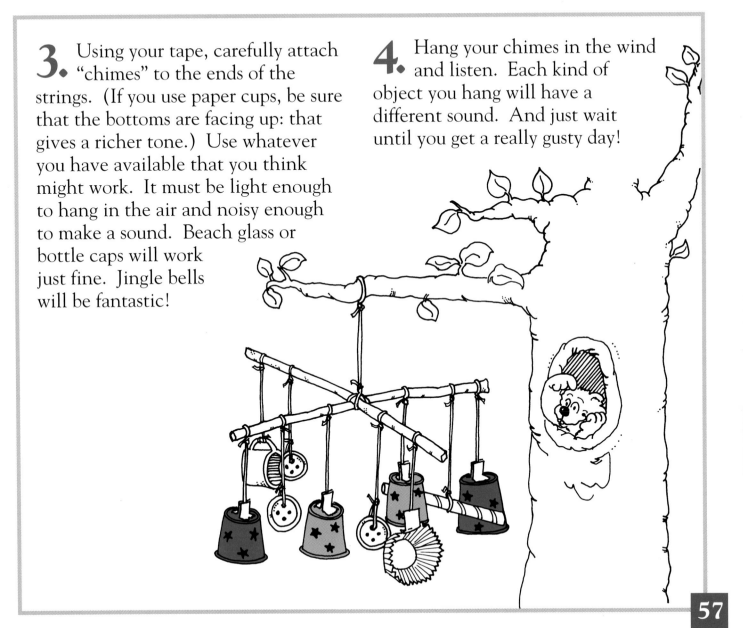

Words for the Weatherwise

Here are some wonderful books to read as part of your Puddle-Jumping fun.

Cloudy with a Chance of Meatballs by Judi Barrett. What would happen if food dropped from the sky instead of rain and snow? Read this funny book and find out!

Katy and the Big Snow by Virginia Lee Burton. When so much snow falls that even the snowplows are stuck, Katy, who is a tractor, comes to the rescue by shoveling out the town.

Where Does the Butterfly Go When It Rains? by Mary Garelick. A good story with wonderful drawings by Leonard Weisgard.

The Big Snow by Berta and Elmer Hader. Ever wonder how forest animals survive in the winter? Read this book to find out.

The Snowy Day by Ezra Jack Keats. Peter has fun in a snowy world.

Peter Spier's Rain by Peter Spier. How does a rainy day feel? This book shows you.

Storm in the Night by Mary Stolz. When a storm comes, Thomas hears a story about his grandfather being afraid.

Rain Rain Rivers by Uri Shulevitz. A girl waits inside on a rainy day, thinking about what she will do when the rain stops.

White Snow, Bright Snow by Alvin Tresselt. A beautiful book about how amazing a snowfall really is.

Crossword Puzzle

Use what you've learned about weather to complete this challenging puzzle.

Across

1. A thermometer measures the
   _____.
3. On a cold day you need to be
   careful of _____ conditions.
5. Snow falls in this kind of shape.
7. These clouds are the puffy,
   "cotton ball" clouds.
8. The star that heats the earth.
9. The water _____ is a
   balance in nature that has been
   going on for millions of years.
10. Jack _____ might nip your
   nose, or the plants in your garden.

Down

2. Kids who love all kinds of
   weather.
4. This will help keep the rain
   off of your head.
6. A _____ passing by might
   give you a minute of shade.

Rhyming Puzzle

All of these words have a rhyming partner that has to do with the weather.
Draw a line from the word to its picture. Good luck!

example: Lost   Frost _____

1. Loud _____

2. Snake_____

3. Bicycle_____

4. Train_____

5. Throw_____

6. Fun_____

7. Cuddle_____

8. Frightening_____

Rhyming Puzzle (above): 1. cloud 2. flake 3. icicle 4. rain 5. snow 6. sun 7. puddle 8. lightning

Down 2. puddle jumpers 4. hat 6. cloud

Crossword (page 59):   *Across* 1. temperature 3. wind chill 5. flake 7. cumulus 8. sun 9. cycle 10. frost